California
Bar
Examination

Essay Questions
and
Selected Answers

February 2012

ESSAY QUESTIONS AND SELECTED ANSWERS
FEBRUARY 2012
CALIFORNIA BAR EXAMINATION

This publication contains the six essay questions from the February 2012 California Bar Examination and two answers to each question that were written by actual applicants who passed the examination after one read.

The selected answers were assigned good grades and were transcribed for publication as submitted, except that minor corrections in spelling and punctuation were made for ease in reading. The answers are reproduced here with the consent of their authors.

FEBRUARY 2012
ESSAY QUESTIONS 1, 2 and 3

California
Bar
Examination

Your answer should demonstrate your ability to analyze the facts in question, to tell the difference between material and immaterial facts, and to discern the points of law and fact upon which the case turns. Your answer should show that you know and understand the pertinent principles and theories of law, their qualifications and limitations, and their relationships to each other.

Your answer should evidence your ability to apply law to the given facts and to reason in a logical, lawyer-like manner from the premises you adopt to a sound conclusion. Do not merely show that you remember legal principles. Instead, try to demonstrate your proficiency in using and applying them.

If your answer contains only a statement of your conclusions, you will receive little credit. State fully the reasons that support your conclusions, and discuss all points thoroughly.

Your answer should be complete, but you should not volunteer information or discuss legal doctrines which are not pertinent to the solution of the problem. Unless a question expressly asks you to use California law, you should answer according to legal theories and principles of general application.

Question 1

Sam, a widower, set up a valid, revocable *inter vivos* trust, naming himself as trustee, and providing that upon his death or incapacity his cousin, Tara, should be successor trustee. He did not name any additional trustee. He directed the trustee to distribute the income from the trust annually, in equal shares, to each of his three children, Ann, Beth, and Carol. He specified that, at the death of the last of the three named children, the trust was to terminate, and the remaining assets were to be distributed to his then living descendants, by representation.

When he established the trust, he also executed a valid will pouring over all his additional assets into the trust.

Two years later, Sam died. He was survived by Ann, Beth, and Carol. Within two months, Dave, age 25, began litigation to prove that he was also a child of Sam's, although Sam had never known of his existence.

For three years after Sam's death, Tara administered the trust as trustee. Because Ann had very serious medical problems and could not work, and because Beth and Carol had sufficient assets of their own, Tara distributed nearly all of the trust income to Ann and little to Beth and Carol.

After the court determined that Dave was in fact Sam's child, Dave claimed a share of the trust. Beth and Carol have filed suit against Tara, claiming breach of fiduciary duties. Tara has submitted her resignation, and Beth and Carol have sought termination of the trust so that all assets may now be distributed outright to the beneficiaries now living.

1) What interests, if any, does Dave have in the trust assets? Discuss. Answer according to California law.

2) Are Beth and Carol likely to be successful in terminating the trust? Discuss.

3) Are Beth and Carol likely to be successful in suing Tara? Discuss.

Question 1
Answer A

1) <u>Will Substitute</u>

Where an inter vivos trust is created, and where the settlor gives a vested future possessory interest in the trust to a grantee, it will be considered a will substitute. Where the settlor has included a clause whereby all of the settlor's assets at the time of his death pour in to the trust for the benefit of the beneficiaries a pourover will is created. The Will requirements must be established to make this valid.

Here, Sam (S) created a valid inter vivos trust, with himself as Trustee and Tara (T) as the successor Trustee for the benefit of his three children Ann (A), Beth (B), and Carol (C). S also provided that at his death all of his other assets should be poured over into the trust for the benefit of A, B, and C.

Therefore, a valid pourover will was created, with each A, B, and C receiving equal shares of all of the assets.

<u>Dave's (D) right as an omitted child</u>

In general, a child may be disinherited if the child is left out of a will or other testamentary document created by a parent. However, where a child is unknown to the parent at the time the testamentary document is created, and the parent had no reason to know of the child, that unknown child will not be disinherited, and will be able to recover his intestate share of the parent's estate. A child's intestate share in a modern per stirpes system, which is the majority view taken, will be an equal share split at the first level of inheritance, in this case among the children.

Here Sam (S) set up the trust only 2 years ago. D was 25 years old at the time of S's death. Because S was born before the execution of the trust and pourover will, he would generally be treated as disinherited and unable to recover. Here, however, S

5

was unaware that D was alive or that D was his child at the time the testamentary documents were created. D would be considered an omitted child and have a right to his intestate share. Because A, B, and C were all alive, D would be entitled to 1/4 of S's estate. Because the trust contained all of the assets of S due to the pourover will, this will be where the assets are taken from. Notwithstanding the clause in the trust that requires the assets to be distributed to living descendants, by representation after A, B, and C die, D will not be required to wait for A, B, and C to die before recovering.

Therefore, D will be entitled as an omitted child to 1/4 of the Trust assets.

2) Termination by B and C

The power of termination depends on whether or not a trust is revocable or irrevocable. An irrevocable trust is created where the intent of the settlor is to make it as such. Here S expressly stated that the trust is to last until the death of the last of the three named children. The majority view is to find in favor of irrevocable trust, so it is likely that this language will be sufficient to establish an irrevocable trust.

Therefore, an irrevocable trust has been established, and the rules of termination, discussed below, will regard such.

Termination of irrevocable trust

Termination of an irrevocable trust can be done, either when the settlor and all of the beneficiaries agree while the settlor is still alive, or if all of the beneficiaries agree and it will not frustrate the purpose of the trust, or a merger where the trustee has become the sole beneficiary. An irrevocable trust is created when the express language of the settlor states as such.

Here, although T has not acted according to the will, and has distributed nearly all of the trust income to A and little to B and C, there must still be a mutual agreement between the beneficiaries to terminate that doesn't frustrate the purpose of the trust. The trust specifically stated that the trust was to be terminated only at the death of the last of the three named children. Just because B and C are unhappy with the way the trust is being distributed does not give them the right to terminate the trust, either without the consent of A, or in the face of clearly stated terms of the trust made by the settlor.

Therefore, B and C will likely not be successful in terminating the trust, but as discussed below may have damages due from T.

3) Type of trust established

To a certain extent a trustee's ability to use discretion varies depending on the type of trust that is established. The greatest deference is given to the trustee in two situations, either a support trust or a discretionary trust. Both of these types of trusts, generally, must expressly state that this is the type of trust being established. The purpose of the trust, which is a necessary requirement of a valid trust should determine what type of trust is created.

Here, the T was instructed to distribute in equal shares annually. There was no express statement of purpose that the trust was being set up for distributions based on the discretion of T, nor based on the need for support of A, B, and C. One of these things would have to be established in order to create a special kind of trust that would give T additional discretionary power.

Therefore, the trust is an express trust, neither discretionary nor support, and T will be bound to the fiduciary duties of a trustee discussed below.

Fiduciary duties of trustee breached by T.

A trustee has a number of duties to the beneficiaries of the trust. Among those duties are a) a duty of care, b) a duty to distribute benefits in accordance with the trust, c) a duty to treat beneficiaries equally, d) and a duty to follow the settlor's instructions. Only in certain circumstances is the trustee allowed to use discretion in how to distribute the income of the trust, namely a discretionary trust or a support trust. The trust duties to the beneficiary are triggered by a trustee accepting their position as such. Where a trustee has breached their fiduciary duties, they may be held personally liable, and/or may be removed from their position by the court. There are additional remedies not pertinent to this case.

Here, S was the original trustee of the trust and named T as the successor trustee. T either expressly, or at the least by conduct, accepted the position as trustee, and therefore was bound by the duties of a trustee to the beneficiaries of the trust.

Therefore, T owed the duties discussed below to A, B, and C, and any breach of such could result in personal liability and/or expulsion from the trustee position.

a) Duty of care

A trustee has the duty to act as a reasonably prudent person in her dealings as trustee. This includes investing reasonably, making reasonable distribution, and all other activities that a trustee conducts in her role as trustee.

Here, T was distributing nearly all of the trust income to A and very little to B and C. A, however, had a very serious medical problem and could not work, while B and C had sufficient assets of their own. The trust however expressly stated that distribution of the income from the trust annually should be in equal shares to each of A, B, and C.

Notwithstanding the express direction given to T as to distribution it is possible that T may have reasoned that S was not aware nor could he foresee the circumstances of A, B, and C and his real purpose was to ensure that the children were taken care of during their lives.

Therefore, T may have been reasonable in her actions as trustee, but it may be a close call because of the express direction given in the trust. T would likely have to use extrinsic evidence to show that she was acting in accordance with S's real purpose.

b) <u>Duty to distribute in accordance with the trust</u>

A trustee has a duty to distribute in accordance with directions given in the trust instrument. This duty is breached when the trustee acts in a way inconsistent with the specific instruction set forth by the settlor.

Here the trust expressly stated to distribute the trust in equal shares annually to A, B, and C. T, however, decided unilaterally to distribute the majority of the trust income to A and very little to B and C. This was clearly inconsistent with the directions given by S in the trust instrument.

Therefore, T breached her duty to act in accordance with the trust, and will be liable to B and C for the difference between what they were distributed and what they were entitled to under the trust.

c) <u>Duty to treat beneficiaries equal</u>

A trustee should give the same care and deference to each beneficiary of the trust, in accordance with the trust purpose.

Here, T gave sympathy to A because of her medical condition, and was less concerned with B and C because they had "sufficient assets of their own." It is not a fair and equal treatment to penalize a beneficiary because they have assets available to them outside of the trust. To hold that such action by a trustee is allowed, would be to disgorge the settlor of the trust of his ability to leave trust assets to whomever he might choose. A trust is not only set up for individuals who are in need (as discussed above this is not a support trust), but rather for the benefit of whomever the settlor feels he would like to distribute benefit to.

Therefore, T has not treated B and C the same as A and will be liable for a breach of duty, again with the remedies as described above.

d) <u>Duty to follow settlor's instructions</u>

A trustee has a duty to follow the instructions given to him be the settlor.

Here, the instruction was to distribute the shares equally to A, B, and C. T did not, as discussed above, do so.

Therefore, T breached his duty to follow instructions of the settlor.

Question 1
Answer B

1) Dave's Interest in the Trust Assets

Pretermitted Children

Dave was not specifically provided for in the trust instrument set up by Sam. This is because the trust only mentioned Ann, Beth, and Carol. As such, Dave would normally not have any interests in the trust. However, a pretermitted child may be entitled to a stake in the trust if he can show that he is a pretermitted child. A pretermitted child is one who is born or discovered after the execution of a will. In this case, Dave was presumably not born after the execution of the trust and will as he was 25 years old at the time of Sam's death, and Sam executed the trust and will only two years before his death. However, [he] had never known of Dave's existence. Therefore, Dave is a pretermitted child of Sam's, and may be entitled to some of Sam's estate.

A pretermitted child is entitled to what would be his intestacy's share of the deceased's estate. A pretermitted will not be entitled to this share of the estate, however, if the deceased specifically excluded all children from his will, and the intent to do so is shown on the face of the document. That is not the case here, though, as Sam created the trust to distribute income to his three children that he knew about. Additionally, a pretermitted child will not be entitled to any interest in the estate if the deceased provides for the child in another manner, such as an inter vivos trust, that is intended to take the place of the child's intestatacy share. Again, this did not happen here because the inter vivos trust did not provide for Dave. Therefore, because Dave is a pretermitted child, and because none of the exceptions apply that would exclude him from having an interest in the deceased's estate, he is entitled to receive what would have been his intestate share of the estate.

Dave's intestate share of the estate would be equal to 25% of the estate. This is because when Sam died, he had four children and was a widower. Also, there is no mention that Sam had any living siblings or parents. All four of Sam's children survived him, and therefore if Sam had died intestate, each child would receive his share based on a per capita calculation. Therefore, each of Sam's four children would be entitled to 25% of his estate if he had died intestate. The calculation of what Dave is entitled to receive will include the value of the trust. This is because the estate is considered to include assets held by the deceased in a revocable inter vivos trust. Here, the trust that Sam created was revocable and inter vivos declaration in trust. Dave will be able to receive his interest in the estate by abating what was given to the other children. This abatement will occur by operation of law, and would mean that Ann, Beth, and Carol would each have their interest reduced from 1/3 of the estate to 25%.

2) Termination of the Trust

There are several manners in which a trust can be terminated. A trust will be terminated when a specific condition in the writing calls for the termination of the trust and is satisfied. In this case, the trust stated that it would terminate at the death of the last of the three named children. Here, all three of the named children are still alive, and therefore the trust will not terminate.

Further, a trust can be terminated when the stated purpose of the trust has been satisfied and all beneficiaries and trustees agree to end the trust. In this case, this option does not appear to be available. Although there was no stated purpose to the trust, it provided for equal payments to each of Sam's children. Therefore, the purpose of the trust appears to be to provide for Sam's children as long as they are living. This purpose is not satisfied as all three children are still living, and can still be provided for. Also, it is not clear that all the beneficiaries would agree to terminate the trust. Only Beth and Carol are suing to terminate the trust, and there is no indication that Ann or Dave would agree to the termination.

In addition, a trust may also be terminated when all beneficiaries agree to terminate the trust. As stated above, it is not clear that all beneficiaries would agree to terminate the trust because there is no indication that Ann or Dave would agree. Also, the trust has further beneficiaries besides the three named children. The trust provides that after the death of the last of the three named children, the remaining assets of the trust were to be distributed to Sam's then living descendants. This is a vested remainder subject to an open class. The class is vested because it is not subject to any conditions precedent, and it is created in an ascertainable group of people (Sam's living descendants). The interest does not violate the rule against perpetuities, which states that for an interest to be valid, it must vest within 21 years of some life in being at the creation of the interest. Here, the interest will vest when the last of the three named children dies. Therefore the interest must and will vest within 21 years of a life in being at the creation of the interest. Because this class has an interest in the trust, they are beneficiaries of the trust. If the trust is to be terminated due to consent of all the beneficiaries of the trust, they must also consent. There is nothing to indicate that they would consent to the termination of the trust, and therefore Beth and Carol will not be successful in terminating the trust.

Beth and Carol may additionally claim that the trust should be terminated because Tara, the sole trustee, resigned from her position, and because the trust itself does not name any additional trustees. However, this argument will be unsuccessful. Courts will not allow a private express trust to fail for lack of trustee. Instead, a court will merely appoint a new trustee. Here, even though the trust itself does not provide for any additional trustees, the court will appoint someone else to serve as trustee rather than letting it fail.

3) Fiduciary Duties of a Trustee

Beth and Carol will likely be successful in suing Tara, as she has breached several of her duties as the trustee. A trust creates a fiduciary type relationship with respect to property that is held by the trustee for the benefit of beneficiaries. The trustee must satisfy those fiduciary duties, and if she fails to, may be personally liable for all losses or damages that result to the trust.

Duty of Loyalty

A trustee must satisfy the duty of loyalty by acting in good faith and in the best interests of the trust and beneficiaries. A trustee must not act for her own benefit. Further, a trustee must not favor certain beneficiaries over others. Here, Tara did nothing to show that she was acting for her own benefit. However, Tara was favoring Ann over the other beneficiaries. Tara was doing this because Ann had serious medical problems and could not work, and because Beth and Carol had sufficient assets of their own. Despite her good motives for acting such, though, Tara still violated her duty of loyalty. Her actions specifically favored Ann over the other two beneficiaries. Further, her actions violated the explicit instructions that were contained in the trust and required her to distribute the income from the trust annually and in equal shares to each of the children. Therefore, Beth and Clara could successfully show that Tara breached her fiduciary duty with respect to the trust.

Duty of Care

Additionally, a trustee must satisfy a duty of care by acting in good faith as a reasonably prudent person would with respect to the trust. Here, Tara failed to follow the explicit instructions contained in the trust that required she distribute the income in equal shares to each of the children by providing nearly all the income to Ann. This failure to follow explicit instructions shows that Tara was not acting as a reasonably prudent person would act with respect to the trust. Rather, a reasonably prudent person would follow the instructions contained in the trust. Therefore, Beth and Carol could show that Tara had also breached her fiduciary duty of care.

Other Duties

It is possible that Tara violated other fiduciary duties, such as the duty to invest, the duty to provide accountings to the beneficiaries, the duty to label trust funds, and the duty to keep trust funds separate from other funds. However, the facts do not indicate that Tara breached any other fiduciary duties she had with respect to the trust.

Remedies

Having violated her fiduciary duties, Tara may be personally liable to the beneficiaries. Beth and Carol could sue Tara for damages of the amount of income that they should have been receiving under the trust. In the alternative, Beth and Carol could sue to have a constructive trust created from the excess income that Ann received over what she was entitled to receive from the trust. In such a scenario, Ann would hold the excess income as a constructive trustee, and would be required to return it to Beth and Carol.

Question 2

City recently opened a new central bus station.

Within the central bus station, City has provided a large bulletin board that is available for free posting of documents. City requires that all free-posted documents be in both English and Spanish because City's population is about equally divided between English- and Spanish-speaking people.

City refused to allow the America for Americans Organization (AAO) to use the bulletin board because AAO sought to post a flyer describing itself in English only. The flyer stated that AAO's primary goal is the restriction of immigration. The flyer also advised of the time and place of meetings and solicited memberships at $10 each.

Does City's refusal to allow AAO to use the bulletin board violate the rights of AAO's members under the First Amendment to the U.S. Constitution? Discuss.

Question 2 Answer A

Free Speech

Under the 1st Amendment as applied to the states via the 14th A, all persons have the right to free speech. While this right is not absolute, there are only certain instances when the government may infringe upon this right.

Strict Scrutiny

America for Americans Organization (AAO) will argue that strict scrutiny should apply. Normally when a government actor limits or regulates speech based on its content, it will have to survive strict scrutiny analysis. Under this, a law will only upheld if it is necessary to achieve a compelling government interest.

AAO will claim that the city is a government actor so the protections of the 1st A will apply. Further, they will say that the law regulates the content of their speech—that it must include parts in Spanish. The court will probably not agree because it is not regulating what they say, rather how they say it. Therefore, it will take it out of strict scrutiny analysis.

Time, Place, & Manner Restrictions

One way a government may validly regulate speech is by controlling the time, place, and manner of the speech. These regulations are put under less scrutiny because they are not limiting what the people can say but rather how and where they can say it.

Public Forum

A public form is a place that is traditionally open to the public and allows somewhat unrestricted speech. These include parks, sidewalks, open fields. The bus station bulletin boards are likely not considered a public forum.

Limited Public Forum

Limited public forums are not traditionally open to public speech, but the government opens them up to the public. Therefore, they receive the treatment of a public forum while open.

AAO will claim this is a limited forum because the boards, while not traditionally open to public speech, are open here to post documents for free. The court will likely agree.

While open to public speech, a limited public forum may only regulate the time, place, and manner of speech if:

1. Content neutral
2. Alternative channels of communication are available, and
3. Regulations are narrowly tailored to achieve a significant government interest.

1. Content Neutral

As mentioned, AAO will claim that the requirement that all posted documents be in both English and Spanish is a regulation based on the content of the speech. The city will claim it is content neutral because it doesn't matter exactly what you say, just how you say it. City will claim this regulates the manner of the speech.

AAO may counter by saying that since the organization has a primary goal of restricting immigration, the regulation goes to the content of their speech because they're speaking out and trying to make it clear that everyone in America should speak/read English. The court may agree with this point but will likely side with the city because the overall requirement that docs be in English and Spanish is not regulating content of the docs but rather the manner in which their speech is conveyed.

Therefore, the regulation is likely content neutral.

2. Alternative Channels

City will also likely show that AAO has other channels of communication available. They can post on other boards or directly hand out fliers. The English/Spanish requirement appears to only apply to this bus station's bulletin board.

3. Narrowly Tailored to Further Significant Interest

City will also argue that this final element is satisfied. They will say they have a significant interest in communicating with and including the Spanish speaking population, which make up about ½ of the people.

Because it is necessary to communicate with your residents, the court may agree with City that this is a significant interest. AAO may argue that City may have a significant interest in relaying government communications, but its interest shouldn't expand to private communications. Further, the burden it would impose on everyone to translate communications into Spanish would be immense, AAO will say.

Even if the court finds the interest in communicating significant, AAO will say this regulation is not narrowly tailored to it. They'll say they could achieve this in other , less restrictive ways, like making communications around heavily populated Spanish speaking areas be in both English/Spanish.

Narrowly tailored means a tight fit. However, because this is a central bus station, it is likely that many Spanish speaking people use it and therefore need the translation.

Therefore, so long as the court finds this regulation is content neutral and is narrowly tailored to a significant gov interest, it will likely be able to refuse to post AAO's flyer for not being in Spanish.

NonPublic Forum

The city may also try to argue this is a nonpublic forum, where speech has traditionally been able to be severely limited. Such places include military bases, airports, and gov buildings. The court has also found a bus advertising signs to be nonpublic.

City will argue this isn't like the inside of a bus where people cannot escape looking at the ads because this is at the station where they could just leave. Court will agree.

Gov can regulate speech in nonpublic forums [as] long as it is reasonable and viewpoint neutral.

Here, the law is likely reasonable due to the ½ Spanish speaking population. Also it is viewpoint neutral because it doesn't discrim on only one side of a viewpoint. It applies to all communications.

Commercial

City may also try to argue this is commercial speech so they can regulate more. That speech can be regulated if not false/misleading, directly advances substantial gov interest, and narrowly tailored into it.

However, even though it seeks membership, City denied it because not in Spanish too.

QUESTION 2
Answer B

Justiciability: In order for a matter to be justiciable there must be standing, the case must be ripe, and not moot. Here, AAO has not filed suit yet, however, it must have standing to raise any objections to the city's requirements.

Standing: standing requires that there be an injury in fact, causation and redressability. Here, AAO is injured as it cannot post its flyers in English only, without potential reprimand. Moreover, the city requirement directly causes its injury, and a court decision in favor of AAO would remedy it. However, an organization will not have standing unless 1) its members have individual standing 2) the interest is germane to the purpose of the organization, and 3) neither the remedy nor the claim would require individual member participation. Here, an individual member who would want to post only flyers in English would have standing, the interest is germane to the purpose of the organization as its primary goal is to restrict immigration and therefore, posting flyers in Spanish would be against its interest and finally, neither a claim or remedy by AAO would require individual member participation.

Ripeness: a court will not award pre-enforcement review for purposes of an advisory opinion. Here, the city has already implemented these requirements. It is unclear whether it is an actual ordinance, regulation or law, but assuming that there are reprimands for violating the city requirements, then the issue is ripe, as AAO would be violating the city requirements if it only posted the flyer in English.

Mootness: there must be a dispute at all times of the litigation. Here, if the city removed its requirement during the litigation the matter would be moot. However, because the city would be free to apply the restriction again whenever it wants there [sic] matter is not moot.

Government conduct: in order for there to be a constitutional violation, there must be government conduct. Here, the city is implementing the requirement; therefore there is government conduct.

First Amendment: the government may not restrict an individual's or organization's freedom of speech unless the speech is not protected or less protected.

Content-Based Restrictions: if a law restricts speech based on its content, whereby it is based on the subject matter or viewpoint of the speech, strict scrutiny review applies. The government must show that the law is necessary to achieve a compelling state interest and it must be the least restrictive means of accomplishing its purpose. Here, AAO will argue that the law is content-based, because it is only allowing flyers that are posted in Spanish and English, and therefore, it is restricting the AAO's message against immigration which would require only posting flyers in English, as posting flyers in Spanish would communicate to the Hispanic community, which is an immigrant population. This is a very far stretched argument. It does not appear that the restriction is based on the subject matter or viewpoint of the speech. AAO could post the same flyer in Spanish stating that its primary purpose is to restrict immigration and advise of the time and place of meetings. Therefore, this argument will fail.

Content-Neutral Restrictions: if a law is content-neutral, then the government must show that the law is substantially related to an important government purpose and is narrowly tailored. As discussed above, the restriction is not content-based, rather, it is content-neutral. The city will argue that the restriction is substantially related to the purpose of communicating to all individuals in its population. The city's population is about equally divided between English and Spanish speaking people, and therefore it is has an important purpose of making sure that messages posted on the board for free will be communicated to all its population. Moreover, the city has narrowly tailored the restriction by not requiring that people post the flyers in multiple languages, but only in two. A court will likely uphold the restriction.

Prior Restraint: if a law restricts speech prior to its communication there is a prior restraint and strict scrutiny applies. The law must be reasonably, narrowly tailored, and definite. Moreover, the government must seek a prompt injunction, and there must be a prompt determination of the validity of the law. Here, AAO will argue that this restriction is a prior restraint on speech. It will argue that because it is required to post flyers in two different languages and expend the money to have the English flyer translated into Spanish it is a prior restraint on speech. As discussed above, however, the restriction is not a prior restraint on speech. The restriction is allowing speech; however, it is requiring that it be posted in two different languages. This is not a prior restraint because it is not prohibiting speech.

Vagueness: a restriction is unconstitutional if it is vague and a reasonable person could not understand the type of speech that is being regulated. Here, the restriction is not vague; it is requiring that all free-posted documents be in both English and Spanish. Therefore, the restriction is valid.

Overbroad: the restriction is unconstitutional if it restricts more speech than is constitutionally allowed. Here, the restriction is not overbroad because it is only requiring free-posted documents to be in both English and Spanish; therefore, it is valid.

Symbolic Speech: the government may restrict symbolic speech when it is narrowly tailored to achieve an important state interest, and it is not directed at the suppression of speech. The burden of proof is on the government. Here, posting flyers will be deemed symbolic speech as they communicate a message. As discussed above, the government will argue that it has an important state interest because it want its entire population to understand the flyers that are posted. The restriction is narrowly tailored as it is only requiring the flyers to be in the languages that are dominant in the population, and the restriction is not directed at the suppression of speech. Rather, it provides the opportunity of communicating to the entire population. AAO will argue that the speech is directed at the suppression of speech, because it is directed at the suppression of AAO'S message against

23

immigration. However, this argument will likely fail as AAO can communicate this same message of its purpose in restricting immigration in Spanish; therefore, the restriction would not suppress AAO's message.

Public Forum: public forums are areas which the constitution requires that the government open to speech. These areas typically includes [sic] parks and sidewalks. Here, the restriction is taking place within the central bus station, wherein the city has provided a large bulletin board that is available for free posting of documents. Because the bulletin board is within the central bus station which is likely government owned this forum will not be deemed a public forum, as it is not a constitutionally required forum for the government to open up to speech. Nevertheless, if it were to be considered a public forum the following analysis would apply:

When there is a content-based restriction the government, strict scrutiny applies, and the government must show that the restriction is necessary to achieve a compelling state interest and it is the least restrictive means of accomplishing its interest. Here, as discussed above it is unlikely that the court will rule this restriction to be content-based, because it is not regulating the subject matter or viewpoint of the language.

When the restriction is content-neutral and is a time, place and manner restriction, the government has to show that the restriction is narrowly tailored to achieve an important state interest and leaves open alternative channels of communication. Here the city will argue that it is only regulating free-posted documents and it is only regulating the manner in which it is posted by requiring it to be in English and Spanish. The city will argue that it has an important purpose in making sure that all its population can understand the message on the board, and it is narrowly tailored to achieve that purpose by only requiring that the free-posted documents be in Spanish and English. Furthermore, it leaves open alternative methods of communications because it is not restricting any speech, but rather it is requiring more speech.

Designated/Limited Public Forum: this is a forum which the government is not required to open up to speech, but it has chosen to open up to speech regardless. The same analysis as the public forum applies as to designated public forums. Content-based speech must pass strict scrutiny, while in content-neutral speech the government has to show that the restriction is narrowly tailored to achieve an important state interest and leaves open alternative channels of communication.

It is likely that the bulletin board within the central bus station will be considered a designated public forum. The government is not required to place a bulletin board in the bus station for organizations and individuals to post flyers, nor is it required to open the central bus station to speech at all; nevertheless it has chosen to do so.

When there is a content-based restriction the government, strict scrutiny applies, and the government must show that the restriction is necessary to achieve a compelling state interest and it is the least restrictive means of accomplishing its interest. Here, as discussed above it is unlikely that the court will rule this restriction to be content-based, because it is not regulating the subject matter or viewpoint of the speech. AAO can get the same message across in both languages.

When the restriction is content-neutral and is a time, place and manner restriction, the government has to show that the restriction is narrowly tailored to achieve an important state interest and leaves open alternative channels of communication. Here the city will argue that it is only regulating free-posted documents and it is only regulating the manner in which it is posted by requiring it to be in English and Spanish. The city will argue that it has an important purpose in making sure that all its population can understand the message on the board, and it is narrowly tailored to achieve that purpose by only requiring that the free-posted documents be in Spanish and English. Furthermore, it leaves open alternative methods of communications because it is not restricting any speech, but rather it is requiring more speech.

Nonpublic forum: A nonpublic forum is a forum wherein the government may constitutionally restrict speech. These include military bases, sidewalks next to a post office, ad space on buses, and solicitation for money in airports. The restriction, however, must be viewpoint neutral and must pass the rational basis test. Here, AAO would have to argue that the restriction is not rationally related to a legitimate government interest.

The city will argue that the central bus station is a nonpublic forum and that the government must not open it to speech. Although the central bus station is likely to be deemed a nonpublic forum, the city has changed the status of the forum by providing a large bulletin board and making it available for people to post their flyers and messages. By doing so the city transformed the public forum to a nonpublic forum. However, the city may also argue that because AAO is soliciting money ($10 for its membership) that it is a nonpublic forum as it can restrict speech of solicitation for money in bus stations as it can in airport. However, this argument is unlikely to apply since AAO is not directly soliciting money by standing at the central bus station and asking for money, rather, only if individuals show up at the time and place of the meeting would it ask for membership fees. At that point, the government would be unable to regulated [sic] the speech. Nevertheless, assuming that the court would deem that this is a nonpublic forum, which it will not, the following analysis would apply.

AAO would argue that the law is not rationally related to a legitimate purpose. However, the city can easily counter this by arguing that its purpose is to have its entire population be able to read the flyers. Therefore, AAO's argument will fail. AAO will then argue that the restriction is not viewpoint neutral as it restricts only anti-immigration speech and not pro-immigration speech. This argument will again fail, as AAO can post the same message of anti-immigration in both languages and it would not deter its purpose. Therefore, AAO would not prevail under this argument.

Freedom of Association: the government may not punish individuals for joining any association unless the individuals knows of the 1) unlawful purpose of the association, 2) the individual actively participates, and 3) the individual intends to advance the illegal purpose. Here, AAO's primary goal is the restriction of immigration. This is not an unlawful purpose; therefore, the government may not punish anyone for their freedom to associate with the AAO. AAO will argue that it is violating its freedom of association by restricting its message. It will argue that the requirement is unconstitutional because the AAO is an intimate association and it would chill its expressive activities. However, this argument is unlikely to prevail as argued above, because AAO's message of anti-immigration can be communicated in multiple languages and would not violate its freedom of association rights.

Equal Protection/Substantive Due Process: AAO would also have potential argument under the equal protection and substantive due process clause of the 14th Amendment. The equal protection requires that the government afford its citizens and organization equal protections of the law. If the law does not discriminate against a suspect or quasi-suspect.

Question 3

Paul sued David in federal court for damages for injuries arising from an automobile accident.

At trial, in his case-in-chief, Paul testified that he was driving westbound, under the speed limit, in the right-hand lane of a highway having two westbound lanes. He further testified that his passenger, Vera, calmly told him she saw a black SUV behind them weaving recklessly through the traffic. He also testified that, about 30 seconds later, he saw David driving a black SUV, which appeared in the left lane and swerved in front of him. He testified that David's black SUV hit the front of his car, seriously injuring him and killing Vera. He rested his case.

In his case-in-chief, David testified that Paul was speeding, lost control of his car, and ran into him. David called Molly, who testified that, on the day of the accident, she had been driving on the highway, saw the aftermath of the accident, stopped to help, and spoke with Paul about the accident. She testified further that, as soon as Paul was taken away in an ambulance, she carefully wrote down notes of what Paul had said to her. She testified that she had no recollection of the conversation. David showed her a photocopy of her notes and she identified them as the ones she wrote down immediately after the accident. The photocopy of the notes was admitted into evidence. The photocopy of the notes stated that Paul told Molly that he was at fault because he was driving too fast and that he offered to pay medical expenses for anyone injured. David rested his case.

Assuming that all appropriate objections and motions were timely made, should the court have admitted:

1. Vera's statement? Discuss.

2. The photocopy of Molly's notes? Discuss.

Answer according to the Federal Rules of Evidence.

Question 3
Answer A

I. VERA'S STATEMENT

The first issue is whether or not Vera's statement to Paul claiming that the black SUV behind them was weaving recklessly through the traffic. Evidence is admissible if it is logically and legally relevant and not subject to any restrictions in the federal rules of evidence.

A. Relevance:

Logical Relevance: Evidence is logically relevant if it tends to prove any fact of consequence in the trial more or less probable. Here, Paul is suing David for injuries arising from an automobile accident. A central issue in this case will be who was at fault for the automobile accident that caused the injuries. The fact that David drives a black SUV and the fact that Vera observed a black SUV weaving recklessly through traffic tends to prove that David was driving recklessly and therefore was at fault for the accident. This evidence is logically relevant.

Legal Relevance: If evidence is logically relevant than [sic] it also must be legally relevant. Legal relevance is determined by whether the evidence is more prejudicial than probative. This requires a balancing test. Here, the evidence is probative because as mentioned it illustrates how one of the parties in this case was driving before the accident. David will argue that it is prejudicial because Vera called him "reckless" and that this statement might cause a jury to cast judgment on his driving. A judge will determine that the probative value outweighs any slight prejudice this evidence may include and is therefore legally relevant.

A court may also exclude evidence that is not legally relevant because it would waste time or confuse the jury. However, this evidence does not require any additional time to be spent to prove additional elements and is not confusing to a jury.

B. Lay Opinion:

David will argue that the statement should be inadmissible because it contains a lay opinion as to the nature in which he was driving his vehicle. Lay opinions are admissible evidence if they are (1) helpful to the jury and (2) do not require any special analysis. Here, if Paul is suing on a negligence theory, David might argue that Vera stating that he was driving recklessly is allowing the witness to testify as to an element of the cause of action. However, David will be successfully [sic] in arguing that Vera could easily see the car driving and that her expression that the car is driving recklessly is merely her opinion on how the driver was swerving through lanes. This evidence will be rendered inadmissible because it is a lay opinion.

C. Hearsay

Paul will argue that Vera's statement is inadmissible because it is hearsay. Hearsay is an out-of-court statement offered to prove the truth of the matter asserted. As a general rule, hearsay is inadmissible because the validity of out-of-court statements is questionable and unreliable. Hearsay is inadmissible unless a valid exception applies. David will argue that the following exceptions apply:

(1) **Present Sense Impression:** A present sense impression is when someone makes a statement about an event they are perceiving at the moment. Present sense impressions are exceptions to the hearsay rule, because they are presumed to be reliable. When someone makes a present sense impression, they have no motivation to lie or misstate what is actually occurring. The facts state that just 30 seconds after Vera made this statement that a black SUV hit Here [sic], Vera simply stated at the time of observing the black SUV that she saw that SUV weaving recklessly through traffic. Therefore, it will be admissible as a present sense impression.

(2) **Present State of Mind:** Another hearsay exception are statements made by individuals that express their current state of mind. Here, Paul will argue that when Vera made the comments about the SUV, she was expressing what she thought

and felt at the time. This statement would also be admissible under the Present State of Mind exception.

(3) **Excited Utterance**: Paul may argue that the excited utterance exception applies as well. An excited utterances [sic] is a statement made at the time of a shocking or exciting event that is made before the shock or excitement as [sic] worn off. Here, David will argue that the swerving of an SUV was not a shocking or exciting event. Further, the facts state that Vera calmly told Paul about the SUV which illustrates that she was not under the shock or excitement of any event. Therefore, the excited utterance exception does not apply.

(4) **Prior Statement:** Prior statements made by individuals that are unavailable to testify sometimes qualify as an exception to the hearsay rule. However, the federal rules of evidence require that the prior statement be made under oath in the course of some type of previous testimony. This statement was made in the car to Paul and is therefore not a valid exception under the prior statement rule.

(5) **Dying Declaration**: Paul may attempt to argue that Vera's statement qualifies under the Dying Declaration exception. This exception states that under some circumstances, statements made under the impression of impeding death are valid exceptions to the hearsay rule. However, the federal rules of evidence state that these statements are only admissible in criminal homicide cases. Moreover, the statement was not made with the knowledge of impending death because the car had not been hit yet and Vera did not know that she might be dying soon. Therefore, it would not qualify under this hearsay exception.

(6) **Federal Catchall Exception**: The federal rules of evidence also allow a catchall exception for statements that are made under circumstances of trustworthiness. Paul will argue that Vera did not have any motivation to lie or to make this information up because it happened at the time of the accident. He will also argue that because Vera is dead there is no other way for this evidence to be admitted for trial. The judge would likely not apply the federal catchall exception because the Present Sense Impression exception is a stronger argument, and you only need one valid exception to admit the evidence.

In conclusion, Vera's statement would be admissible evidence as a present sense impression.

II. PHOTOCOPY OF MOLLY'S NOTES

The issue here is whether or not the photocopy of Molly's notes that state that Paul told her he was at fault because he was driving too fast and that he offered to pay medical expenses can be admitted into evidence.

A. Capacity to Testify:

A witness may testify if she has personal knowledge of the event in question, she recalls the event in question, she has the ability to communication [sic] these perceptions, and she takes an oath to tell the truth. Here, Molly has personal knowledge of the facts perceived because she was there the day of the accident, saw what happened, and remembers that she took notes describing the day's events. While she does not recall the events at this moment, this can be satisfied in other ways that are discussed below. She has the ability to communicate and presumably took an oath prior to testimony.

B. Authentication of Document

Before any documents or other types of recordings are entered into evidence, they must be authenticated and the proper foundation must be laid. Here, Molly has testified that she was there on the day of the accident and they [sic] she remembers that she carefully wrote down notes of what Paul had said to her. Therefore, there is a foundation for the photocopy of the notes. Moreover, David showed Molly the copy of the notes while she was on the stand and she identified them as the ones that she took that day. This would suffice as authentication.

Documents being admitted into evidence are also subject to the Best Evidence Rule. The Best Evidence Rule states that if a document is going to be admitted into evidence, then the original must be produced or the party must account for why the original cannot be produced. The federal rules of evidence have accepted photocopies of documents as satisfying the best evidence rule.

Therefore, the document has been properly authenticated and a photocopy will suffice as a representation of the original.

C. Relevance

Logical Relevance: (See rule statement above.) Here, Paul's statements are logically relevant. They tend to prove whether or not Paul was at fault in the accident more probable than not. Whether or not Paul was at fault or not is a fact of consequence to this case since a central issue is who was at fault to the accident.

Legal Relevance: (See rule statement above.) These statements are more probative than prejudicial. There are not statements that might prejudice Paul because they are statements that Paul himself stated.

Offer to Pay Medical Expenses: However, there are some types of evidence that are not admissible for public policy reasons under the rule of legal significance. For example, evidence of insurance, subsequent remedial repairs, and offers to settle are inadmissible because as a society we want to promote people to carry insurance, rectify dangerous situations, and settle cases as not to clog the courts. Another such category is when one party offers to pay the medical expenses of the other party. Here, there are two statements that Paul made. The first is that he was at fault because he was driving too fast. The second is his offer to pay medical expenses for anyone injured. The ferenda rules of evidence will sever these two statements. Because the offer to pay medical expenses is inadmissible but the other statements made in connection with the offer are admissible.

D. Dual Hearsay:

(See rule statement above.) The issue with the photocopy of Molly's notes is that there are two levels of hearsay. In order for a document that contains two levels of hearsay to be admissible evidence, there must be valid exceptions for both statements.

a. First Level of Hearsay: Paul's Statements.

The first level of hearsay is Paul's statements that he made to Molly. These statements were made at the scene of the accident presumably and thus are out of court statements. David will argue that the following exceptions apply:

(1) Party Admission: An admission made by a party to the case is admissible because under the federal rules, it constitutes non-hearsay. Here, Paul admitted fault to the accident. He stated that he was driving too fast and explicitly said that he was at fault. Thus, this is a valid party admission and would be admitted as non-hearsay.

(2) Statement Against Interest: Another category of non-hearsay is when a party makes a statement against interest. Statements against interest are any statements that an individual makes that are against his pecuniary interest. Here, stating that one is at fault for an auto accident would be a statement against his interest. Therefore, this exception would apply.

b. Second Level of Hearsay: Molly's notes

The second level of hearsay is the notes that Molly wrote down on the paper. Molly wrote those notes on the day of the accident and not while in the courtroom. Therefore, the notes are Molly's out-of-court statements. David will argue that the evidence should be admitted because of the following two exceptions:

(1) Prior Recollection Recorded: Courts will admit prior recollection recorded if four elements are met. First, the witness must currently not be able to recall the facts that are in the writing. The facts state here that Molly testified that she has no recollection of the conversation. The second is that the writing be created by the witness or adopted by the witness. Here, Molly herself wrote down the notes. Third, the writing must have been made when her memory was still fresh. Here, Molly created the writing as soon as Paul was taken away in the ambulance; therefore, we can assume that her memory was still fresh. Fourth, the writing must have been made under reliable conditions. Here, there is no evidence of an alternative purpose that Molly created the writing except for the document [sic] the events as they occurred. If all of these elements are satisfied, the recollection may be read into evidence; however, the photocopy should not be admitted into evidence.

(2) Present Recollection Refreshed: A party can refresh a witness' memory with virtually any document. Therefore, if Molly did not recall the events, David could have shown Molly the document and allowed her to look over the writing. If this refreshed her memory, then she could testify as to her knowledge of the events. In this situation, the writing would normally not be entered into evidence unless the opposing party suggested that it be admitted. However, this does not apply because Molly was shown the document, but then did not review it or subsequently answer questions based off of her review.

In conclusion, the photocopy should not have been entered into evidence because even though there were valid hearsay exceptions applied, the appropriate way to admit the evidence would have been to read the evidence into the record as opposed to giving the jury the photocopy.

Question 3
Answer B

The case between Paul in [sic] David is a civil case, which means there are a few different rules than when you are in a criminal case. This case is about injuries arising out of an automobile accident in which Paul is suing David. At issue is going to be who is at fault for the injuries and the accident.

1. Did the court err in admitting Vera's statement?

Vera's statement was made while she was a passenger in the car with Paul on the day of the accident. She stated in a calm manner that she saw a black SUV behind them weaving recklessly through the traffic.

Logical Relevance

All evidence must be relevant to be admissible. This includes tending to prove or disprove a fact that is of consequence. Even if evidence is relevant it may be inadmissible if it is not legally relevant.

Here, Vera's statement is being offered to prove the identity of a vehicle that she observed driving recklessly, which is the same vehicle that David drives. It is also relevant to prove that Paul had notice/was aware of the black SUV driving radically. Additionally, it is relevant to prove that David was at fault and was driving recklessly.

So although Vera's statement has logical relevance its probative value must be determined.

Legal Relevance

Evidence that is logically relevant may be excluded if it will create an unfair prejudice. The court has discretion as to whether or not to exclude the evidence. The test to determine whether the evidence should be excluded on a legal relevancy ground is whether the unfair prejudicial effect substantially outweighs the probative value.

Here, the prejudicial effect will be that David will be determined to have driven recklessly by weaving in and out of traffic. However, this is highly probative and is what is at issue and being determined in the case, so Vera's statement will not be excluded on grounds of legal relevance.

Even relevant evidence that is otherwise admissible can be inadmissible when it is in violation of one of the federal rules of evidence.

One of the objections that David could make regarding the admissibility of this evidence, besides relevancy, would be hearsay.

Hearsay

Hearsay is a rule which prevents out-of-court statements from being admitted into evidence, if the statement is being offered for the trust of the matter asserted. The reason hearsay evidence is prohibited is because it was not subject to cross-examination and cannot be determined if the statement was fabricated or reliable. Since the information in Vera's statement about a black SUV driving recklessly would be helpful to a jury or trier of fact and is being offered to prove that the reckless driving of the SUV did in fact take place it is being offered for its truth and should be excluded unless a hearsay exception or exemption applies.

Hearsay Exceptions

Hearsay exceptions are statements that are made out of court and are admitted for their truth but we allow them in for other reasons. Here, Paul will try and argue that Vera's statement should get in under several different exceptions.

Present Sense Impression

A present since impression is an exception to hearsay because it is considered to have reliability given the fact that the statement is made while or immediately after perceiving an event. There seems to be little time to fabricate a statement when it is made while you are perceiving it.

Here, Paul is going to argue that Vera made the statement while still in the car when she saw the black SUV weaving recklessly through traffic. She was currently perceiving the SUV driving in such a manner and made the statement while making the observation. It is of no matter that she made the statement calmly because this does not negate that she had just observed the SUV driving recklessly.

David might try and counter that Vera did not make the statement immediately when she observed the car driving recklessly, but there are no facts to support that she didn't make the statement while she was observing. Also statements are allowed to be made immediately after observation, because there is still the indication that there is not time to fabricate. Absent any facts showing that Vera waited any amount of time after observing the SUV driving recklessly and telling Paul this statement could come in under the present sense impression.

Excited Utterance

Excited utterance allows hearsay evidence to come in if the statement was made while under the stress or effect of an exciting or startling event. Here, Paul might try and claim that Vera commented on the SUV's reckless driving while she was still under the stress of the observation. However, David will have a valid argument against this contention because Vera calmly told Paul about the SUV and did not seem to be effected by it in a manner to justify an excited utterance.

Former Statement

Former statements can be admitted as long as the declaring is unavailable. Unavailability of a declaring can be because of death, not able to locate after reasonable attempts, and/or incapacity. Here, Vera is dead so she is unavailable. Former statements that are made under oath at a previous proceeding can be admitted for impeachment purposes and to prove the truth of the matter asserted. Here, Vera's statement was not made under oath at a formal proceeding and could only be used for impeachment. However, since there is no one to impeach because Paul is offering his case and chief [sic] as a plaintiff, thus going first, this statement cannot be admitted as a former statement even though Vera is unavailable.

Dying Declaration

Dying declarations are allowed in criminal homicide cases as well [as] civil. Here, we are in a civil case so a dying declaration is allowed as long as the declaring is unavailable, they do not have to actually die, they made a statement regarding the cause of their death, and they made the statement under the belief that death was impeding or imminent. Here, there is no valid argument to support that Vera's statement was a dying declaration since she made the statement prior to Paul's car being struck by the black SUV and prior to her death. Even though Vera is now unavailable she did not make a statement thinking she was going to die or describing the cause of her death and this exception is not available for Paul to get Vera's statement admitted.

Personal Knowledge

Personal knowledge is required for a witness to be able to testify as to an event. While Paul did not personally observe the black SUV driving recklessly as Vera did, he did perceive Vera's statement with one of his 5 senses and thus has personal knowledge that the statement was made and the manner in which it was made.

Hearsay Exemptions

These statements are not hearsay because they are not admitted to prove the truth of the matter and are admitted for a different purpose. Here, Paul is going to argue that Vera's statement should come in as non-hearsay under several different grounds.

Effect on the hearer

Effect on the hearer is not being offered to prove the truth of the matter and thus is not hearsay. This is offered to show the effect the statement had on the person hearing the statement. Here, Paul could assert this statement is being offered to show that Paul was aware of a black SUV that was driving recklessly. Since Paul's driving is also being put at issue by David this is important for Paul to prove that he was on alert of the black SUV driving recklessly that struck him 30 seconds after hearing the statement from Vera.

Conclusion

Because this statement could fall under the present sense impression exception and effect on the hearer exemption to hearsay this statement cannot be excluded on hearsay grounds and the court properly admitted Vera's statement.

2. Did the court err in admitting the photocopy of Molly's notes?

Logical/Legal Relevancy

Molly's notes are relevant to prove that Paul made a statement accepting fault and offering to pay medical bills. They are being offered by David for this matter and to prove that it is true as well. Although relevant to determine fault the evidence must also not be unfairly prejudicial.

Policy reasons to exclude relevant evidence

Certain evidence although relevant will be excluded because of public policy reasons. Courts want to encourage parties to fix wrongs, settle cases, and help each other out. Here, Paul will argue that the notes should be excluded because they were an offer to pay medical bills. Offers to pay medical bills cannot be offered to show fault of a party.

Although offers to pay medical bills of the injured [sic] is not allowed into evidence under the federal rules of evidence, the FRE severs statements made in connection with the offers and allows them into evidence. Here, Paul made the statement that he was driving too fast, was at fault, and offering to pay medical expenses of anyone injured.

The statements regarding Paul driving too fast and being at fault will not be excluded under this policy reason but may be excluded on other grounds (see discussion below).

Error in allowing an offer to pay medical expenses

So in regards to the court allowing in a photocopy of a document that included the offer to pay medical expenses there is an error because public policy seeks to keep these sorts of statements excluded.

The statement regarding Paul driving too fast and being at fault

The photocopy of Molly's notes being admitted constituted a recorded recollection and is actual evidence being admitted. All tangible, physical, non-testimonial evidence that is being admitted must be authenticated in order to be admitted.

Authentification

Here, Molly is on the stand claiming that she wrote the notes immediately after the accident and that the notes are hers. This is sufficient to authenticate the notes because Molly is claiming they are what David purports them to be and she is on the stand and capable of being questioned as to the notes' authenticity.

Refreshing Recollection

Anything can be used to refresh a witness's recollection. Here, David is attempting to use notes to refresh Molly's recollection. Witnesses must be shown whatever is attempting to refresh their recollection in order to see if the item is successful in helping them recall. Whatever is used to refresh a witness's recollection may be offered into evidence by the opposing party.

Here, it is not Paul offering the notes used to refresh Molly's recollection into evidence; it is David, which means he is attempting to offer the notes as a recorded recollection.

Paul may argue that Molly was not given the notes before claiming that her memory failed and thus the rules regarding admitting record recollection evidence were not followed. Generally a witness should be given the document to review silently and then if they still cannot remember the document may be admitted into evidence. Paul may have a valid argument here since the facts do not say that this was done. It appears from the facts that Molly before even reviewing the document said she couldn't remember, then it was moved into evidence.

Record Recollection

Documents offered into evidence that were used to refresh a witness's recollection are permitted so long as the witness's memory has failed to be refreshed, the witness is on the stand and able to be crossed and authenticate the document, the witness accurately prepared the document close in time to perceiving the events, and had personal knowledge of the thing to which they recorded information about.

Here, Molly did testify that she was unable to recall the conversation. She is on the stand and subject to cross and questioning. And she testified that she carefully wrote down the notes as soon as Paul was taken away in the ambulance; additionally she had personal knowledge of the conversation with Paul since she heard the conversation herself. Given these facts David would be able to properly admit the evidence as record recollection as long as no other restrictions exist permitting the admissibility of the evidence.

Best Evidence Rule

The Best evidence rule is a rule which calls for the document itself to be admitted when someone is on the stand trying to testify as to the contents of the document. Here, Molly is trying to recall a conversation and the notes contain information about the conversation. Since the notes are her own memory and not of legal significance the best evidence rule does not apply.

However, Paul will try and assert that there is a problem with the best evidence rule as well as authentification because the actual note itself was not admitted and a photocopy was admitted. Paul will try and argue that unless David can show a justifiable reason why a photocopy of the note and not the actual note was admitted there is a problem/violation with the best evidence rule. David will successfully counter that argument by claiming that a photocopy, properly authenticated, is an acceptable document to satisfy the best evidence rule.

Hearsay/ Multiple Hearsay

See rule above and discussion above. Here we also have a case of multiple hearsay since there is a statement within a document both made/prepared out of court and being offered for the truth of the matter asserted. So both the statement and the document must meet their own separate hearsay exception or exemption. As discussed above the document itself can get in under the record recollection rule but there needs to be an exception for the actual statements.

Party Admission-

Party admissions are considered non-hearsay and are statements offered by a party opponent made by the other party. These statements do not have to be against interest necessarily but they must be made by one party and offered by the other. Here David is attempting to offer statements that Paul made, and although not required, are against his interest and regard his fault in the accident. This could be a valid ground for admitting the statements made by Paul.

Statement against interest

David may try and assert that the statements made by Paul can come in under a statement against interest exception to hearsay. However, this exception requires that the declaring be unavailable which is not the case here, since Paul is the plaintiff in the matter and is available in court.

Conclusion

The court was likely proper in admitting the evidence because the document can come in under the record recollection and the statement is admissible as a party admission.

FEBRUARY 2012
ESSAY QUESTIONS 4, 5 and 6

California
Bar
Examination

Answer all three questions.

Your answer should demonstrate your ability to analyze the facts in question, to tell the difference between material and immaterial facts, and to discern the points of law and fact upon which the case turns. Your answer should show that you know and understand the pertinent principles and theories of law, their qualifications and limitations, and their relationships to each other.

Your answer should evidence your ability to apply law to the given facts and to reason in a logical, lawyer-like manner from the premises you adopt to a sound conclusion. Do not merely show that you remember legal principles; instead, try to demonstrate your proficiency in using and applying them.

If your answer contains only a statement of your conclusions, you will receive little credit. State fully the reasons that support your conclusions, and discuss all points thoroughly.

Your answer should be complete, but you should not volunteer information or discuss legal doctrines that are not pertinent to the solution of the problem.

Unless a question expressly asks you to use California law, you should answer according to legal theories and principles of general application.

Question 4

Testco, Inc. conducts market surveys, and is solely owned by Amy, Ben, and Carl. Each paid $50 for one-third of Testco's no-par shares. Amy and Ben, respectively, are Testco's president and secretary and its only two directors. Carl holds no office and is not involved in any aspect of Testco's business. Amy and Ben are scrupulous about holding directors' meetings to conduct corporate business and to make monthly distributions to the shareholders of almost all cash on hand. As a result of the latter practice, Testco has little cash on hand and frequently finds itself in the position of negotiating extensions for payment of its debt.

While Ben was on vacation, Examco called Amy, asking to enter into a one-year contract with Testco. Amy said that if Examco would agree to a ten-year contract, Testco would grant its standard fifty-percent discount. Examco agreed, and Amy signed the contract in the following manner: "Testco, by Amy, President." When Ben returned, he said that he had thought for some time that Testco's standard fifty-percent discount was unwise, and convinced Amy to revoke the contract with Examco.

Examco wants to sue Testco, Amy, Ben, and Carl for damages. If found liable, Testco will not be able to pay.

On what theory or theories may Examco bring an action for recovery of damages against:

1. Testco? Discuss.

2. Amy, Ben, and Carl as individuals? Discuss.

QUESTION 4
Answer A

Examco v. Testco

Breach of Contract

If Testco is to be found liable to Examco, it will be on a breach of contract theory. Breach of contract occurs where there is a valid contract, a breach, and then damages as a result of the breach. A valid contract exists when there is an offer, acceptance, consideration, and no defenses to contract formation.

Here, Examco asked Amy to enter into a ten-year contract, which Amy then signed on behalf of Testco. Amy agreed that in consideration for the length of time of the contract, that she would give Examco a fifty percent discount. Thus there was a valid contract between both Examco and Amy on behalf of Testco.

A breach of the contract occurred when Amy anticipatorily repudiated the contract between the two companies. It is likely that Examco will receive damages as a result of not getting the benefit of their bargain with Testco; thus there is a valid action for breach of contract. However, Testco will only be bound to this contract if Amy had authority to enter into the agreement with Examco (see below).

Agency

Agency is where a principal with capacity manifests assent that an agent act on behalf of the principal for its benefit and subject to its control followed by the agent manifesting assent to do the same. Here, Amy as president of Testco was an agent of the company since she was appointed to the position of president (assent), working for the benefit of the company, and subject to the control of the board of directors. Thus

Amy was an agent of Testco and Testco will be liable on the contract with Examco if she had some form of authority to enter into the contract.

Amy's Authority

A principal is liable on the contracts entered into by their agent on their behalf so long as the agent has authority. Authority can come in three forms: actual authority, apparent authority, and ratification.

Actual Authority

Actual authority is the authority that the agent reasonably believes that they have based upon the manifestations of the principal. Actual authority can be express or implied.

Express Actual Authority

Express actual authority is the authority given from the four corners of the agency agreement.

Here, there is no agency agreement between Amy and Testco; however, there is probably some sort of express manifestation of assent in the bylaws or articles of incorporation of Testco. Usually in the corporate setting, when a contract such as this is entered into, the board of directors will usually vote to pass a resolution to give the president of the company the authority to enter into the contract. However, there was no such board resolution here since Amy did not consult with Ben prior to signing the contract. Since there are no facts going to express authority, a different form of authority must be found to bind Testco to the contract with Examco.

Implied Actual Authority

Implied actual authority is the authority that the agent reasonably believes that they have based upon necessity in order to carry out their express authority, customs of the position held by the agent, and by prior dealings with the principal.

Here, Amy, as president of Testco, would likely have implied actual authority to enter into the Examco contract by virtue of her position as president of the company. Presidents of corporation[s] customarily have the authority to enter into binding contracts with other companies. Additionally, it is necessary for a president to enter into contracts with other companies in order to make the corporation profitable. Making the corporation profitable is a duty of the president of the company and thus it is necessary that Amy entered into this contract in order to fulfill that duty.

Testco will argue that, although Amy was president and had authority to enter into smaller contracts, this contract was different in the fact that it went ten years into the future and that Amy was giving such a huge discount. Testco will argue that this sort of contract required express board resolution and thus Amy could not have reasonably believed to have authority to enter into it. However, the facts state that Amy gave the "standard fifty-percent discount;" thus it seems like this was a regular occurrence of the corporation to enter into contracts of this nature. As such there was implied actual authority.

Apparent Authority

In the event that the court finds that there was no actual authority, they could find apparent authority to bind Testco to the contract. Apparent authority is the authority that a third party reasonably believes that the agent possesses based upon the manifestations of the principal. One form of manifestation by the principal would be the position that the principal has placed the agent in is a position that is usually associate[d] with the grant of authority.

Here, Examco can successfully argue that Amy had apparent authority do [sic] to her title of president of Testco. When they were entering into the contract they dealt directly with the president of the company. Additionally when the contract was signed, it was signed "Testco, by Amy, President". As such, it would have been reasonable for Examco to believe that Amy had apparent authority to enter into the contract.

Ratification

Another form of authority is ratification. Ratification occurs where after the agent has entered into a contract, the principal has knowledge of it and accepts its benefits. Here, when Amy told Ben about the contract, he told her to immediately revoke it. Thus there was no board resolution ratifying the contract with Examco and there will be no finding of authority based upon ratification.

Conclusion

Since there is at least the finding of apparent authority on behalf of Amy for Testco, Testco is bound to the contract with Examco and will be liable to them on a theory of breach of contract.

Examco v. Amy, Ben, and Carl as Individuals

Liability of Shareholders

Shareholders of a corporation are only personally liable for the cost of their shares of stock in the corporation. They are not personally liable for the corporation's debts, liabilities, or obligations. Thus, Amy, Ben, and Carl will not be liable to Examco personally unless the corporate veil can be pierced (see below).

Piercing the Corporate Veil

In order to recover from the personal assets of the shareholders of Testco, Examco will have to make a sufficient showing to pierce the corporate veil. The corporate veil is pierced based upon a variety of factors. These factors include whether there was fraudulent conduct by the shareholders, whether the corporation is undercapitalized, whether the corporation is simply an alter ego of the shareholders, and whether the creditor of the corporation is an involuntary creditor.

Fraud

Fraud is the misrepresentation of a material fact known to be false with the intent to induce some action upon another where the other suffers damages. Here, the facts do not suggest that Amy made any misrepresentations when entering into the contract with Testco; thus a pierce of the corporate veil will not be achieved on the ground of fraud.

Alter-Ego

A corporation acting as the alter ego of the shareholders will be found where the shareholders forgo the usual formalities of corporate status. Here, Testco has officers and a board of directors; however, the facts state that Amy and Ben are "scrupulous" about holding director's meetings to conduct business. Thus it could be seen that they have foregone the formalities of a usual corporation. Thus this factor weighs in favor of a pierce of the veil.

Undercapitalization

Undercapitalization of a corporation occurs where the corporation does not keep enough surplus cash on hand in order to pay the foreseeable liabilities of the corporation. Here this factor weighs heavily on favor of piercing the veil since all of the extra cash on hand was distributed to the shareholders. It was foreseeable that eventually a contract would be breached or some mistake would be made causing liability on behalf of Testco. Thus since there was not enough cash on hand to pay the liability to Examco, the veil may be pierced.

Involuntary Creditor

An involuntary creditor is usually a tort victim or tort judgment holder. Here, Examco had every opportunity to inspect records and the financial security of Testco prior to entering into the contract. Thus they were not an involuntary creditor.

Carl's Liability

Usually a shareholder that is uninvolved with the daily operations of the company will not be held liable as a result of veil piercing. Here, Carl did not participate in any of the activities of Testco except to receive distributions from the company. Thus he may or may not be held liable to Examco.

Conclusion

The factors presented above weigh in favor of piercing the corporate veil; thus Examco may go after the shareholders of Testco, with the possible exception of Carl.

QUESTION 4
Answer B

The remedies that are available to Examco for Testco revocating their agreement depend on the legal status of the agreement and whether Amy had the authority under agency principles to bind Testco to the agreement if it can be legally enforced. The agreement concerns money which is proper consideration from Examco to Testco for providing its market survey services. There were negotiations between both parties regarding the price and discount that would be offered as well as the length of the contract. Both parties agreed on the 10 year terms and the 50% discount. Amy signed the contract. This is enough to create a legally enforceable contract if Amy had the authority to enter into contracts on behalf of the corporation — this is determined by principles of agency which I now analyze.

Amy as Agent of Testco

An agent is a person or entity that acts on behalf of another, the principal. For an agency relationship to exist there must be assent by the agent to the existence of the relationship and its duties, the agent must act for the benefit of the principal, and the principal must control the agent's actions on its behalf.

Here Amy is the President of the corporation. She has assented to the relationship by accepting this employment and the duties and privileges (e.g., salary, benefits) that come along with it. She acts for the benefit of the corporation in this capacity. This is because by virtue of her position in the management of the corporation as an officer she has a Duty of Care to the corporation and must act in good faith and as a reasonably prudent person would with his or her own business. Further, in addition to this Duty of Care she also has a Duty of Loyalty whereby she must act in the best interest of the corporation before all others including herself. These duties insure that Amy's actions should be for the benefit of the corporation in all actions she does on its behalf. Third, the corporation itself has control over Amy. This is because Amy is an employee of the corporation and serves at the will of the board of directors and at its direction. Her

52

employment can be terminated at any time by the board or shareholders (by majority vote at a meeting or special meeting).

Because the three prongs of agency have been satisfied, Amy is an agent of the corporation. As such, she may be able to bind the corporation to agreements depending on whether she has the appropriate authority to do so.

Actual Express Authority

Actual express authority is the authority that is expressly given to an agent by a principal for some particular task. This authority can be orally conveyed or it can be in writing. According to the equal dignity rule, if a writing would be required for the transaction or action at issue if the principal were to act directly for himself instead of through his agent, the principal is required to expressly give the agent express written authorization to undertake the action on the principal's behalf.

There is no factual information to suggest that Amy had either oral or written actual express authority to enter into contracts on behalf of the corporation. Further, even if the board or shareholders expressly passed a resolution stating that Amy had such authority, or that the President of the corporation has such authority, the resolution and authorization it granted must be in writing. This is due to the equal dignity rule. Because the contract that was actually signed by Amy called for her firm's services to be rendered over the course of 10 years, the Statute of Frauds requires a signed writing (because performance necessarily will take longer than one year by the terms of the contract). Amy herself signed such a writing. However, there is no evidence to suggest that the board gave her such written authorization.

Thus, Amy did not have actual express authority to enter into the contract on behalf of Testco on the basis of the factual information given. However, she may have had implied authority to do so.

Actual Implied Authority

Actual implied authority is that authority which is necessary for it to carry out its expressly authorized actions and in fact was implied from that authorization, or authority that comes with virtue of the position the agent has with respect to the principal and the duties associated with this position.

Here if Amy had received express authority from the board to manage all sales regarding Testco's service contracts, she would have the implied authority to enter into a contract with Examco at terms that she determined because such authority is necessary to manage all sales of service contracts. However, since there is no evidence of an express authorization this prong of implied authority will not suffice.

The second possibility that will give rise to implied authority is if the agent by virtue of his or [her] position and the duties associated with such a position has authority to enter into a contract. Here Amy has been appointed by the board of directors of Testco as its president. As such, she is the chief executive officer of the corporation and is responsible for overseeing all day-to-day operations of the corporation. By virtue of this position and the duty that comes with it — to manage the corporation — Amy has the implied authority to act on the corporation's behalf in her management of the corporation.

Thus, when she signed the contract with Examco she was acting with the implied authority granted to her by virtue of her position as president charged with management of the company. On this basis, Testco can be held liable for a breach of contract.

Apparent Authority

Apparent authority is the authority that arises when a third party reasonably believes that the agent has such authority because the principal "cloaked" the agent with the appearance of such authority.

Here Amy is the president of the corporation. She holds herself out as such when she entered into the contract with Examco. By virtue of permitting Amy to negotiate such service agreements, which appears to be the case given Ben's objection to the usual 50% reduction, Testco was holding her out to third parties as having the authority to enter into such agreements. Further, Amy signed the contract with Examco as "Testco, by Amy, President." Acting in the cloak of authority given to her by Examco by virtue of her ability to negotiate sales service agreements with customers and by virtue of the apparent authority she has as Testco's president, she had the apparent authority to bind the corporation when contracting with a third party, here Examco, who reasonably believed she had such authority.

Thus, because Amy had the implied authority and apparent authority to enter into this contract on Testco's behalf and she did so, Testco is liable for breach of the contract by its revocation. Examco can seek damages directly against Testco.

2) The determination of whether there is liability for Amy, Ben, and Carl will depend on whether there is director liability for Amy and Ben in their capacities as directors and officers of the corporation. And for all three, Amy, Ben, and Carl based on whether the veil can be pierced for purposes of their limited liability.

Piercing the Veil

Directors, managers, and shareholders are generally not liable for their actions to a third party that is suing the corporation. That is true, unless the corporate veil that insulates them from liability can be pierced. Piercing of the corporate veil is an extraordinary remedy that is only awarded when the directors, officers, and shareholders do not provide for sufficient capital or insurance for the corporation's debts and where the corporation is but an alter ego of the shareholders. The latter can be established in part by the officers and managers not observing sufficient corporate formalities.

Undercapitalization

Directors are not permitted to make a dividend distribution that puts the corporation at risk for insolvency. In fact, the prohibition against this is so strong that the directors will be personally liable for such a distribution unless they believed the corporation was not at risk of insolvency based on the financial officer's report which they are allowed to reasonably rely upon.

Amy and Ben

Here Amy and Ben voted in favor of making monthly distributions that put little cash on hand and leading to the corporation needing to negotiate extensions for payment of its debt. This put the corporation at risk for insolvency because if a large judgment came through or one of its creditors was unwilling to renegotiate its payment terms. Amy and Ben as shareholders and directors did this to benefit themselves at the expense of the corporation. This violated their duty of loyalty to act in the best interests of the corporation above even their own. They did not do this because they held 2/3 of the shares and put the corporation at risk of insolvency merely to line their own pockets with distributions. This would also violate their duty of care to the corporation because they would not put themselves at such risk of insolvency in the management of their personal business. This undercapitalization will lead to Examco likely not being able to recover its damages for breach of its contract. It should be permitted to recover its expectation damage measure, the amount it reasonably expected to profit from the agreement at the time it was entered into.

Courts are more likely to pierce the veil for a tort action than they are for a contract dispute.

Here we have a contract dispute between a corporation and another corporation. It is due to the fact that Amy and Ben determined that the contract would not be profitable. While normally this would not be such an egregious breach, because it may lead to an overall benefit if the breach was efficient, here it is especially so because Amy and Ben have undercapitalized the corporation and there are likely no assets which Examco can reach when it successfully sues. As such, the court should pierce the corporate veil to allow Examco to recover the impermissible cash distributions that Amy and Ben had been awarding themselves and would otherwise be available.

Carl

While Carl is also a shareholder and normally his 1/3 interest in the corporation would be sufficient to raise him to the status of a controlling shareholder, here he does not have such control. Amy and Ben are the only two officers, the only two directors, and when combined they hold a 2/3 interest in the corporation as shareholders. Carl is merely a passive investor that is not involved in any aspect of Testco's business. He merely invested $50 in no-par stock in a venture run by Amy and Ben. As such, while the veil should be pierced for Amy and Ben as to their shareholders' limited liability but should not be for Carl because he committed no improper acts and was merely a passive investor.

Limited Liability

Question 5

Attorney mailed a professional announcement to several local physicians, listing his name and address and his area of law practice as personal injury. Doctor received Attorney's announcement and recommended that her patient, Peter, call Attorney. Peter had become very ill; he thought the cause was breathing fumes from a chemical company near his home.

Attorney agreed to represent Peter in a lawsuit against the chemical company. At Attorney's request, Doctor agreed to testify as an expert witness on Peter's behalf at the trial. Attorney advanced Doctor expert witness fees of $200 an hour for her time attending depositions, preparing for trial, and testifying.

Attorney learned in discovery that numerous scientific studies had failed to find any medical risks from the chemical company's fumes. Doctor was nevertheless willing to testify, on the basis of her clinical experience, that the fumes had harmed Peter. Attorney did not know whether Doctor's testimony was true or false. He offered Doctor's testimony at trial, and Peter won a judgment.

After the trial, Attorney sent a $500 gift certificate to Doctor, with a note thanking her for recommending that Peter call him.

What, if any, ethical violations has Attorney committed? Discuss.

Answer according to California and ABA authorities.

QUESTION 5
Answer A

What, if any, ethical violations has Attorney committed?

The attorney may be liable for ethical violations for: 1) mailing a professional announcement to physicians in the area, 2) paying an expert witness fee, 3) allowing the doctor to testify, and 4) sending the doctor a gift.

Mailing a Professional Announcement to Physicians in the Area

Both the ABA and California prohibit in person, live solicitation to individuals who the attorney does not have a familial or professional relationship with. However, attorneys are allowed to send professional announcements, letters, cards, etc. to people in the area. Moreover, the document must have certain information contained in it, such as the attorney's name or if it is a firm, a name of one attorney in the firm. It must also have an address listed for the attorney and/or any other relatable contact information. However, the document must be accurate and fair, the attorney is not allowed to guarantee success rates or hold himself out as a specialist unless he is certified by the proper authorities in the state.

Here, the attorney is not soliciting in person and is rather sending professional announcements to physicians in the area. This is not prohibited by the ABA or California rules. Furthermore, the attorney has included his name and address as well as his practice of law. The announcement is not misleading and is the accurate reflection of the attorney's information. Moreover, it is of no consequence that the doctor referred her client to the attorney. The attorney and the doctor have not set up a referral service and are not sharing in any of the fee. The doctor simply referred her injured client to the attorney based on the announcement she received. Therefore, the attorney will not be in violation of any ethical rules for sending out professional announcements.

Paying an Expert Witness Fee

Both the ABA and California rules permit attorneys to compensate expert witnesses for their time exerted on the case. However, the compensation cannot be hinged on favorable testimony from the witness. The compensation must also be reasonable in light of factors such as the expert's familiarity with the subject, his experience in the field and other similar factors.

Here, the attorney is advancing the doctor an expert witness fee of $200 an hour for her time attending depositions, preparing for trial, and testifying. These are all ethical reasons for the attorney to compensate the expert witness for. There are no facts to indicate that the attorney is paying for favorable testimony or that the fee being paid is unreasonable. Therefore, the attorney has not violated any ethical rules by compensating his expert witness.

Allowing the Doctor to Testify

An attorney is allowed to call witnesses to testify on his client's behalf. However, there are some exceptions to this rule. One major exception to this rule is if the attorney knows that the witness will perjure him or herself. This is also a place where the ABA and California rules differ.

ABA

Under the ABA, an attorney shall not call a witness to testify if the attorney knows the witness will commit perjury. However, if the witness is the defendant in a criminal case he has a constitutional right to testify on behalf of himself. The ABA states that if her client insists on testifying and perjuring herself the attorney must attempt to persuade her not to. If the client still insists on testifying, then the attorney should attempt to withdraw as counsel if the court will allow it depending on how damaging it will be to the client. Finally, if the attorney is unable to withdraw he must carefully weigh the balance of his duty of confidentiality with his duty of candor to the court. If the client persists on testifying then the attorney may advise the court about the perjury.

California Rules

Under California, the rule regarding witnesses who are not the clients are the same. An attorney is prohibited from calling a witness who he knows will perjure himself. However, the California rules differ from the ABA regarding a client who wishes to testify on behalf of himself and who wishes to perjure himself as well. In California, an attorney must make the same effort to attempt to persuade the client to not perjure himself. Furthermore, the attorney must try to withdraw as counsel if the court permits it. The big distinction is that in California an attorney is allowed to let his client testify in narrative fashion regarding the false information. He also is not required to breach is [sic] duty of confidentiality and warn the court of the perjury.

In this Case

Here, the doctor who is testifying is not the client and therefore the attorney under both the ABA and California rules is not permitted to call the doctor if he knows he will perjure himself. The facts state that the attorney learned in discovery that numerous scientific studies had failed to find any medical risks from the chemical company's fumes. Nevertheless, the doctor was willing to testify, on the basis of her clinical experience, that the fumes had harmed Peter. Although the scientific studies failed to find any risks of the fumes, this does not mean that the doctor is necessarily lying. An attorney has a duty to represent his client zealously and just because there is some evidence that states the fumes may not be dangerous there are no facts to indicate that the doctor is lying. The doctor is testifying based on her clinical experience and is allowed to testify even if it contradicts some of the scientific studies. The only way the attorney will not be allowed to call the doctor as a witness is if he knows that she will be committing perjury when she goes on the stand. In light of all the facts, the attorney has not breached any ethical duties by allowing the doctor to testify.

Sending the Doctor a Gift

Both the ABA and the California rules prohibit sending gifts to witnesses who testify on their behalf. The attorney is only allowed to compensate the expert witness for her services in the case such as depositions, preparing for trial and testifying. Moreover, a gift to an expert witness may compromise the witness's ability to be fair and not to give favorable testimony in anticipation of a gift. If the gift was intended for the doctor as a thank you for testifying it will not be allowed.

Referral Fee

Also, an attorney is not allowed to send a gift to a person whether they are a witness or not for referring someone to him. This would be a kickback or a referral service fee. These are explicitly prohibited unless the attorney satisfies certain criteria such as: 1) getting informed consent from the client, 2) having in the contract how the referral is to be split up, and 3) the referral must not be exclusive between the attorney and the referring party.

Here, the attorney has sent a $500 gift certificate to the doctor with a note thanking her for recommending that Peter call him. This violates both the referral arrangement stated above and also violates the ethical rules for compensating an expert witness. Thus, the attorney will be in violation for sending the doctor the $500 gift certificate.

Conclusion

In light of all the facts, the attorney has not violated any rules by his conduct except sending the $500 gift certificate to the doctor, of which he will be found to be in violation of the ethical rules both under the ABA and California.

QUESTION 5
Answer B

Ethical violations committed by Attorney in the representation of Peter (P).

A. Attorney advertising

i The applicable rules

The issue is what limits there are on an attorney's right to send out advertising for her services. The Supreme Court has held that attorney advertising is protected by the First Amendment as commercial speech. While states may prohibit in-person and over-the-phone solicitation entirely, states may only proscribe attorney advertising sent by mail, as it was here if it is either false or misleading. States may impose other regulations as well. For example, in California, all attorney advertisements by mail must announce on the cover of the envelope and on the ad within that this is attorney advertising. It must name an attorney responsible for the ad, as well as the attorney's address. It must list the attorney's area of law practice, and may include information about past results if the attorney makes clear that such results are not typical and that they are not a prediction of future results. A copy of the advertisement must also be held for two years.

ii. Rules applied to A's conduct

In this case, Attorney (A) mailed an advertisement for his services to local physicians. His mailing has First Amendment protection. There is nothing to suggest that the ad was false or misleading. Also, while it is true that the ad will be presumed false/misleading if it is sent to a hospital or some other place where prospective clients may be under undue pressure or distress, there is no indication that A sent the mailing to clients; rather, he sent it to their physicians, who would in such a vulnerable condition [sic]. Thus, A does not have a false or misleading ad, and he will not be liable on that count.

Further, we are told that the ad listed his name and address. However, we are not told whether the advertisement stated on the envelope and on the letter that this was an advertisement. If not, A may have committed an ethical violation.

Therefore, it appears that the mailing does not violate any rules of professional conduct under either ABA or California authorities.

B. Solicitation of prospective clients

i. The applicable rules

As noted, the ABA and California rules of professional conduct prohibit attorneys from soliciting clients for pecuniary gain in person or over the phone. There is an exception where the client and the attorney have an established relationship, are family members, or the client is a corporation.

ii. Rules applied to A's conduct

While none of these exceptions apply in this case, the attorney has not committed any ethical violation because he did not solicit clients over the phone or in person. Rather, he sent a broad mailing. This type of advertising is acceptable and does not constitute a violation of the rules.

C. Paying an expert witness's fees

i. The applicable rules

Under ABA Professional Rules, an attorney may not make any advance payments to a client in anticipation of litigation. Nor may an attorney give loans to the client, even if the client promises to repay. The only exception under the ABA rules is that an attorney may advance the costs of litigation to a client in order to facilitate the client's commencement of a claim. However, under the California Rules of Professional

Conduct (CRPC), attorneys may make loans to clients in anticipation of litigation, as well as fronting any legal costs associated with bringing the claim.

Additionally, clients/attorneys pay compensate an expert witness for his testimony/work so long as the payment is not given in exchange for specific testimony, such as testimony that is favorable to the client's case.

ii. Rules applied to A's conduct

In this case, A has advanced to Doctor (D) an amount of money intended to compensate him for his work as an expert witness. Under the ABA Rules, this probably [does] not constitute a violation of the ethical rules. The costs of hiring an expert witness are high, and many prospective clients would be unable to hire one. However, without the ability to hire an expert witness, the client might not know if he has a colorable claim against the defendant. Thus, advancing the costs of hiring an expert, as A has done here, probably would not violate the ABA Ethical Rules. These are the costs of litigation, and are probably covered under the exception under these rules.

With respect to the CRPC, it is even more likely that advancing D's fees will not constitute an ethical violation. The CPRC makes clear that attorneys may make loans to a client so long as the client has an obligation to pay the attorney back. Here, when Peter (P) wins on his claim, he will have to either pay A for the costs of hiring D as a witness, or the costs will be taken out of any contingency fee awarded to A from P's judgment against the chemical company.

Thus, under both the ABA and California rules, advancing costs to D is not a violation of the ethical rules.

D. Offering D's testimony at trial

i. The applicable rules

There are two sets of conflicting ethical rules that make resolution of this issue somewhat complex. First, A has an obligation to represent his client zealously, in good faith, and to make all colorable claims that support his client's case. This means that A has an ethical obligation to make every argument on P's behalf that A thinks is supported by the record. He should do so only in good faith, but he must be a zealous advocate at all times.

In contrast, all attorneys also have a duty of candor to the court. This means that attorneys should not offer false evidence into the record. Where there is authority that is controlling and on point, the attorney must bring such authority to the court's attention, even if the authority is detrimental to the attorney's position. Attorneys must conduct themselves honestly in court, and may not make any malicious, unfounded claims that the attorney knows have no support in the record.

As noted, these two duties often conflict, and may put attorneys in a precarious position.

ii. The rules applied to A's conduct

In this case, A learned during discovery that numerous scientific studies had failed to find any medical risk from the defendant's fumes. Nevertheless, D, the expert witness who has treated P and was hired by A to prove A's case, believes otherwise. D is willing to testify, on the basis of her experience and knowledge, that the fumes had harmed P. A has offered D's testimony at trial without knowing whether it is true or false. The question is whether this is a violation of A's duty of candor to the court.

In answering this question, it is important to analyze what A knew and didn't know at the time he offered D's testimony into evidence. First, it should be noted that only the studies A found in discovery were able to find no link between the chemicals and P's injury. We are not told whether there may be other studies out there that support such a connection that A has yet to find. In fact, if the list of studies reviewed by A is not exhaustive, there very well may be a study out there that supports such a connection. Second, it is not clear who funded these studies, or whether the authors had some sort of bias that might discredit their findings. Further, we are not told whether this is a field of science that has been closed to further research, or whether it is a relatively new field that is still developing. It is possible that the chemical in question is relatively new, and therefore its consequences are only recently being analyzed/discovered. There might be other scientists (like D) that are using new techniques to study the connection between the chemicals and injuries, but the results just haven't been published yet. In sum, we can conclude that A has very little information that should convince him, one way or another, that D's testimony is false. There are many open questions about the chemical and a possible link between the chemical and P's injuries.

As noted, attorneys have a duty to represent their clients zealously and to make all colorable claims. The facts tell us that A did not know whether D's testimony was false or true, and this makes sense because D was the expert in the field. While it is unethical for an attorney to offer testimony that she knows to be false, there is no ethical problem under either the ABA rules or the CRPC if the attorney merely has doubts. This is especially true in light of the attorney's obligation to her client. The attorney has an obligation to represent her client vigorously. Thus, it would likely be an ethical violation of A's duty to her client were she to not offer D's testimony into evidence. Since A did offer the testimony on P's behalf, and A did not knowingly offer any false evidence in the process, A did not violate any ethical rules with respect to offering D's testimony.

E. Sharing fees with non-attorneys

i. Applicable Rule

Under the ABA rules, an attorney may not share legal fees with a non-attorney. In California, the attorney may share a fee if the attorney discloses the fee-sharing arrangement to the client and the client consents.

ii. The rules applied

In this case, we are told that A contacted D, a non-attorney, with a mailing advertisement, seeking potential clients. At first, there was no arrangement to share any resulting fees with D. However, after A won a judgment for P, he sent D a $500 gift certificate (the certificate). This is arguably an offer from A to D to share the fees from P's case. A was compensated for his work representing P, and presumably the money that paid for the certificate came from these funds. Thus, A has arguably violated the ethical rule against sharing attorney's fees with a non-attorney. However, A will argue that he gave D the money not for D's work at trial, but for D's recommending P to A as a client. While this may free him from a violation under the "sharing-of-fees" rule, it will support an argument that he violated another ethical rule, as discussed immediately below.

Note that had A disclosed the arrangement to P ahead of time, and had P consented, this would not have been an ethical violation under California's ethical rules. However, because A failed to do so, his conduct is a violation of both the ABA and the California rules of professional conduct.

F. Paying for Referrals

i. Applicable Rule

Under the ABA ethical rules, attorneys may not offer money or services in exchange for getting referrals for prospective clients for pecuniary gain. However, in California, the attorney may pay for a referral if the attorney discloses the referral to the client at the outset of contacting the client, and the client consents to the representation despite having this knowledge.

ii. Rule Applied

68

The same facts discussed above in section "E" (compensation for referral) are applicable here. However, as noted above, it is also significant that A included a note with the certificate, thanking D for recommending that Peter call him. This sounds like a tit-for-tat situation, in which A is compensating D for making a referral. Thus, one would argue that A gave the certificate to D as compensation for referring P's case to A. Holding A liable under this rule is just another way of characterizing the gift certificate that was given to D after P won his case. In this scenario, the money was given to D for D's work efore the case began, rather than for D's work during the trial that contributed to P's judgment and A's resulting compensation (as suggested in section "E", supra). As mentioned above, A's note to D supports the argument that the certificate was intended to compensate D for making the referral, which is a direct violation of the ABA and California rules.

Under the California rules, an attorney may compensate [a] third party who referred a client so long as the compensation is disclosed to the client and the client consents to being represented by the attorney. Because A did not get P's consent before sending the certificate, A's conduct violated the ABA and California ethical rules.

Question 6

Donna was looking for a place to live. Perry owned a two-story home, with the second story available to lease.

Donna and Perry signed a two-year lease that provided, in part: "Lessee may assign the leased premises only with the prior written consent of Lessor."

Upon moving in, Donna discovered that the water in her shower became very hot if Perry ran water downstairs. When Donna complained to Perry about the shower and asked him to make repairs, Perry refused, saying, "I'll just make sure not to run the water when you are in the shower."

Perry soon adopted a new diet featuring strong-smelling cheese. Donna told Perry that the smell of the cheese annoyed and nauseated her. Perry replied: "Too bad; that's my diet now."

After constantly smelling the cheese for three weeks, Donna decided to move out and to assign the lease to a friend who was a wealthy historian.

Donna sought Perry's consent to assign the lease to her friend. Perry refused to consent, saying, "I've had bad experiences with historians, especially wealthy ones." Thereafter, every time Donna took a shower, Perry deliberately ran the water downstairs.

After two weeks of worrying about taking a shower for fear of being scalded and with the odor of cheese still pervasive, Donna stopped paying rent, returned the key, and moved out. At that time, there were twenty-two months remaining on the lease.

Perry has sued Donna for breach of the lease, seeking damages for past due rent and for prospective rent through the end of the lease term.

What defenses may Donna reasonably raise and how are they likely to fare? Discuss.

QUESTION 6
Answer A

As set forth below, Donna can raise the following defenses (1) material breach of lease, (2) constructive eviction, (3) breach of the warranty of habitability, and (4) failure to mitigate damages. Donna is likely to succeed on all four defenses.

1. Material Breach of Lease.

Tenancy for Fixed Term.

A fixed term tenancy is a pre-agreed term by the landlord and tenant.

Here, Donna and Perry signed a "two-year lease." As such, the term of the lease is fixed at two years.

Therefore, Donna is obligated to pay rent for the full two years of the lease, unless otherwise excused.

Duty to Repair.

Generally, a tenant has a duty to keep the premises in good order and repair, unless otherwise agreed to by the parties. The landlord, however, has a duty to repair common areas of use.

Here, there was something wrong with the plumbing in Perry's home. Each time Donna took a shower, she was scalded if Perry was taking a shower at the same time. She notified Perry of the problem, but her [sic] refused to fix it — stating only that he would not take a shower while she did. The leased premises is [sic] part of Perry's home. It is not a separate apartment, did not have separate plumbing or other utilities. Even if Donna wanted to fix the problem herself, she would have not have the ability to do so since she did not lease or control the areas of the home that were the source of the

71

problem. Perry controlled these items. The plumbing was, in essence, a common area under Perry's control.

Therefore, Perry, as landlord, had the duty to repair the plumbing issue and breached his duty to Donna by failing to repair it.

Duty re Nuisance.

A landlord owes a duty of quiet enjoyment to his tenant, including the abatement of nuisances to the extent within his control. A nuisance is something that would be offensive to a person of ordinary sensibilities.

Here, Donna was "annoyed" and became "nauseated" at the smell of Perry's new diet of strong-smelling cheese. However, this appears to be something unique to Donna. She was perfectly willing to assign the lease to her friend the wealthy historian - who would have been subjected to the same smell. A friend would not do this to a friend, unless she knew that the problem with the smell was due to her being ultra-sensitive to that particular cheese. As such, this ultra sensitivity does not arise to the level of being a nuisance.

Therefore, Perry did not breach his duty to Donna by failing to stop eating the cheese.

On the other hand, however, Perry began intentionally annoying Donna. After their dispute regarding the cheese and the possible lease assignment, he began to deliberately turn on the water whenever Donna tried to take a shower. This meant that Donna was not able to take a shower for nearly two weeks. Most anyone of normal sensibilities would be annoyed by this behavior.

Therefore, Perry did breach his duty to Donna by deliberately running the water while she took a shower.

Duty to Pay Rent Despite Material Breach.

At common law, a tenant's duty to pay rent is not relieved by the landlord's material breach of lease. Modernly, a material breach of lease that goes to habitability relieves the tenant's obligation to pay rent.

Here, Perry breached the lease by failing to repair the plumbing. He further breached it by deliberately running the water each time she took a shower. Nevertheless, Donna still owed a duty to pay rent to Perry, despite the breach. Under modern statutes, however, Donna will likely be relieved of the obligation to pay rent because the breach went to her use, enjoyment, and habitability of the leased premises.

Conclusion re #1 Breach of Lease.

As such, Perry breached the lease by failing to repair the plumbing. Therefore, Donna can reasonably raise this as a defense and is likely to succeed.

2. Constructive Eviction.

A landlord owes a duty of quiet enjoyment to his tenant. In the event of (a) a substantial interference with the use and enjoyment of the premises, the tenant may (b) give notice to the landlord, and (c) leave the premises, thereby being excused from any further obligations under the lease.

Here, re (a) there was something wrong with the plumbing in Perry's home. Each time Donna took a shower, she was scalded if Perry was taking a shower at the same time. She notified Perry of the problem, but her [sic] refused to fix it — stating only that he would not take a shower while she did. What's more, Perry began intentionally annoying Donna. After their dispute regarding the cheese and the possible lease assignment, he began to deliberately turn on the water whenever Donna tried to take a shower. This meant that Donna was not able to take a shower for nearly two weeks. Most anyone of normal sensibilities would be annoyed by this behavior. Not being able to take a shower in your own apartment is a substantial interference with the use and enjoyment of the apartment.

Therefore, element (a) is met.

Here, re (b) Donna had notified Perry about the problem. At first he said he would simply not run water while she took a shower. However, in the end, he did so deliberately. As such, Perry had notice of the plumbing problem.

Therefore, element (b) is met.

Here, re (c) after two weeks with no shower, she turned stopped paying rent, returned the key and moved out.

Therefore, element (c) is met.

As such, elements (a), (b), and (c) are met. Therefore, Donna is relieved of her obligations under the lease through Perry's constructive eviction.

Conclusion re #2 Constructive Eviction.

Therefore, Donna can reasonably raise a defense of constructive eviction and is likely to succeed with this defense.

3. Breach of Warranty of Habitability.

A landlord of residential property, which includes commercial in California, owes a duty to his tenant to keep the premises fit for normal habitation. This duty is breached when the landlord fails to fix a condition that impacts the habitability of the premises or violates building codes.

Here, Donna was being scalded each time she took a shower. This started out being an unintentional problem, but grew into an intentional problem when Perry used the defect to intentionally annoy Donna. In the end, Donna was unable to take a shower at all for fear of being burned or scalded. The plumbing issue is likely a building code violation as well. Building codes typically set standards for the temperature of water coming from hot water heaters to avoid burning and scalding, as was happening here. Nevertheless, Perry refused to fix it.

Here, regarding the cheese, Donna was "annoyed" and became "nauseated" at the smell of Perry's new diet of strong-smelling cheese. However, this appears to be something unique to Donna. It does not go to the building code or other habitability issues.

Therefore, Perry breached his warranty of habitability to Donna by failing to fix the plumbing.

Remedies for breach of warranty of habitability.

When a breach of the warranty of habitability occurs, a tenant has several option;, the tenant can (a) stay in the premises, deduct rent and repair the issue, (b) stay in the premises and abate rent until the issue is repaired, or (c) stop paying rent and move out.

Here, Donna chose option (c). She stopped paying rent, returned the keys and moved out. Therefore, she is relieved from any further obligation under the lease.

Conclusion re #3 Breach of Warranty of Habitability.

Therefore, Donna can reasonably raise a defense of breach of warranty of habitability and is likely to succeed with this defense.

4. Failure to Mitigate damages.

A landlord has a duty to mitigate his damages in the event of a breach by the tenant.

Here, Donna tried to find another solution for Perry. She wanted to move out and assign the lease to her wealthy historian friend. The lease required consent for this assignment, and Donna was seeking such consent. However, Perry decided he really did not want to live with a wealthy historian because of his prior bad experiences with them. Due to the nature of this [sic] leased premises, that it was a part of Perry's actual home that required the sharing of space, it is not necessarily unreasonable for Perry to be a little picky about this. Nevertheless, Perry did not even agree to meet with the wealthy historian. Being wealthy and [a] historian does not automatically place someone in an annoying class. Perry's prior experience was probably on a personal level with an individual and had nothing to do with him being a wealthy historian. Perry should have, at a minimum, met with the person, interviewed him, sought references, and otherwise done his due diligence before turning down the opportunity. By failing to do this, he failed to mitigate his damages.

Mitigation as limitation on damages.

A landlord has a duty to use reasonable efforts to re-let the premises. Damages will be reduced by an amount found [that] could have been reasonably avoided.

Here, no, after Donna has left the premises, Perry is under a continuing duty to mitigate his damages by using reasonable efforts to re-let the premises. He must advertise it and seek a reasonable replacement for Donna. Perry is not automatically entitled to full rent for the remaining 22 months without first trying to re let the premises. He already knows at least on [sic] prospective tenant — the wealthy historian — who would take Donna's place.

Therefore, Perry's award for damages, if any, will be reduced by the amount that is shown could have been avoided by mitigating his damages.

Conclusion re #4 Failure to Mitigate.

Therefore, Donna can reasonably raise a defense for failure to mitigate damages and is likely to succeed — at least in part — on this defense.

Overall Conclusion.

In conclusion, Donna can raise the following defenses: (1) material breach of lease, (2) constructive eviction, (3) breach of the warranty of habitability, and (4) failure to mitigate damages. Donna is likely to succeed on all four defenses.

QUESTION 6
Answer B

Statute of Frauds

A contract which cannot, by its terms, be completed or fully performed within one year must be in writing in order to be enforceable. Furthermore, a contract conveying an interest in land must be in writing in order to be enforceable. In order to satisfy the statute of frauds, a contract that comes within its purview must be signed by the party to be bound. Here, Donna and Perry have entered into an agreement to lease the second story of Perry's home for two years. Donna has "signed" the lease, meaning it must have been in writing, and she is the party to be bound. Therefore, the statute of frauds will not be an effective defense to enforcement of the contract against Donna.

Valid Assignment

If Donna validly assigned the lease to her friend, then she would only be secondarily liable based on privity of contract with the original leasor, Perry. The original lessor must seek payment from a valid assignee before seeking payment from the assignor.

Lack of Privity of Estate

If the assignment from Donna to her friend is valid, then privity of estate is destroyed between Perry and Donna. However, privity of estate is not required if there is privity of contract between the landlord and previous tenant. Therefore, the lack of privity of estate will not protect Donna from a lawsuit following a valid assignment because, as the original lessee, she still has privity of contract with Perry.

Restriction on Alienation/Assignment

Restrictions on alienation of property are disfavored. As a consequence, lease clauses restricting a tenant's right to assign or sublease will be strictly construed. For example, a prohibition on assignment absent consent will not prohibit sublease without consent and vice versa. Here, the lease prohibits assignment without consent and would not bar sublease. However, Donna sought to assign her interest to her friend. The language is not controlling. The difference between assignment and sublease is whether the whole remainder of the term is conveyed to the new tenant. If the whole remainder of the lease term is conveyed, then the transfer is an assignment. If only part of the remaining term is conveyed, then the transfer is a sublease. Here, Donna sought an assignment.

Landlord's Unreasonable Refusal to Consent to Assignment

Under the terms of the lease, an assignment requires the landlord's prior written consent. Donna sought Perry's consent and he refused because he had "bad experiences with historians, especially wealthy ones." Donna may argue that Perry's refusal was unreasonable and that the assignment should be valid.

In residential leases of a single family dwelling, a landlord's refusal of consent need not be reasonable so long as it is not based on an unlawful form of discrimination--such as race. In commercial leases or residential leases for large apartment complexes, most jurisdictions require the landlord's refusal to be objectively reasonable, but not so with small residential leases such as the second story of Perry's home. Perry discriminated on the basis of Donna's friend's occupation and wealth which are not unlawful bases. Therefore, Perry's refusal is permissible and Donna will not be permitted to avoid liability by assigning her lease to her friend.

Implied Warranty of Habitability

Every residential lease contains an implied warranty of habitability which requires the leased premises to be fit for basic human dwelling. Housing code violations and serious problems such as lack of heat in a cold winter, lack of running water, flooding, etc. would constitute violations of the implied warranty of habitability. A tenant has several options when the implied warranty of habitability has been violated. After giving the landlord reasonable notice, the tenant may repair the problem and deduct the cost from rent payments, may repair the problem and sue for the cost in damages, may remain in possession and sue for damages, or may move out and avoid liability for the remaining rent. Here, Donna wishes to move out which she may do if the alleged violation is sufficiently serious.

Stinky Cheese

The smell of Perry's cheese, though annoying and nauseating, is problably not enough to make the leased premises unfit for basic human dwelling. If Donna's nausea is so severe that the smell constitutes a health risk to her, then her claim would be significantly strong, but that does not appear to be the case here.

Hot Shower

The hot shower water definitely constitutes a safety hazard, but may not, by itself, be enough to make the premises unfit for basic human dwelling. This is a close call. In conclusion, Donna will probably not be successful on a claim for violation of the implied warranty of habitability. She has a strong claim for constructive eviction anyway.

Constructive Eviction

If, by a landlord's act or omission, a tenant is constructively evicted from premises, then the tenant is relieved of any obligation to pay rent. In order to satisfy the requirements for a constructive eviction, there must be (1) substantial interference with the tenant's use and enjoyment of the leased premises, (2) reasonable notice and time to fix or repair, and (3) tenant must vacate within a reasonable amount of time.

(1) Substantial Interference

Meanness--"Too bad; that's my diet now"

As a landlord, Perry is very mean and refuses to express any concern for Donna's comfort. Just because a landlord is mean does not constitute substantial interference with a tenant's use or enjoyment of her property. Therefore, Perry's meanness will not be sufficient to satisfy the substantial interference requirement.

Landlord's Duty to Repair--Hot Shower

A landlord generally does not have a duty to repair defects in leased premises with several exceptions such as a duty to keep common areas reasonably safe and a duty to make safe furnished, short-term leased premises. If there is a risk of serious harm from a latent defect inside leased premises on a long-term lease, however, a landlord has a duty to repair the problem. The tenant must give the landlord notice of the problem. If the tenant gives notice and the landlord refuses or fails to repair the defect, then the landlord has violated his duty. Here, Donna faces a serious latent defect by virtue of the shower being so hot that it could seriously burn her. She notified Perry and Perry refused to repair. He took steps to avoid injury (at first) by "mak[ing] sure not to run the water when [Donna was] in the shower," but he did not repair the defect. This omission, in the presence of a duty to repair, may constitute a substantial interference provided that the risk of injury is sufficiently high.

Retaliation--Hot Shower

A landlord must not retaliate against tenant for complaints or requests made under the lease. Here, Donna merely sought Perry's consent to assign the lease to her friend. Perry refused and, thereafter, deliberately ran the water downstairs to make Donna's shower dangerously hot. This intentional, bad-faith retaliation for requesting to assign her lease to another constitutes substantial interference with Donna's use and enjoyment of the premises because it created a significant risk of injury to her.

Nuisance--Stinky Cheese

A private nuisance is any substantial interference with another person's use and enjoyment of property to which they have a right to possession. Whether an alleged nuisance constitutes substantial interference is an objective question. If the plaintiff is deemed ultra-sensitive, she will not recover because the interference is not objectively substantial even if it is substantial subjectively. Whether the stinky cheese is a substantial interference is a question of fact for the trier of fact at trial. Depending on the severity of the odor, a reasonable person may find that stinky cheese odor constitutes substantial interference. Therefore, Donna may satisfy the substantial interference requirement based on the stinky cheese as well as the retaliation.

(2) Notice

Donna gave Perry notice of the problems with the shower and the stinky cheese as evidenced by Perry's recognition of her complaints. Donna gave Perry a total of five weeks to resolve the problems about which she complained. Perry refused to resolve the issues. Therefore, the notice and time to repair requirements are satisfied.

(3) Vacate

Donna moved out of the premises and returned the keys in a timely manner.

Conclusion--Constructive Eviction Satisfied

Based on the foregoing, Donna has satisfied the requirements for constructive eviction and will not be liable for past due or future due rent for the remainder of the lease. She is not liable for past due rent because she stopped paying at or after the time the constructive eviction arose--namely, when Perry started retaliating after already refusing to repair the hot shower. She is not liable for future rent because she has been constructively evicted and moved out by that time.

Absence of Equitable Defenses

Perry may claim equitable defenses such as laches or unclean hands, but Donna moved out timely and did not have unclean hands. Rather she demonstrated good faith by giving notice and returning the keys and moving out in a peaceable fashion.

Duty to Mitigate/Avoidable Consequences

Even assuming that Donna moved out wrongfully, when a tenant wrongfully vacates premises, the landlord has three options (1) treat the tenant's vacation as a voluntary surrender and accept without demanding further rent, (2) re-let the premises [to] someone else as an act of mitigation and sue the tenant for the unpaid rent, (3) only in a minority of jurisdictions, ignore the tenant's act and sue for damages for past and future due rent. As a general/majority rule, and the rule reflected in the second option, a landlord must attempt to re-let premises in order to obtain damages that would otherwise be considered avoidable. Any damages that could reasonably have been avoided by mitigation will not be awarded to the landlord.

Here, Perry attempted to hold Donna liable for the entire twenty-two months remaining on the lease. None of those money damages are recoverable because Perry could reasonably have avoided those damages by leasing the premises to Donna's friend.

Conclusion

Donna has successful defenses based on constructive eviction and failure to mitigate damages.